Ball games

Jenny Giles
Illustrated by Judith Love

This is
a tennis ball.

This is
a table tennis ball.

5

This is

a hockey ball.

7

This is
a baseball.

9

This is

a basketball.

This is

a soccer ball.

13

This is

a football.

tennis
ball

table tennis
ball

hockey
ball

baseball

basketball

soccer ball

football